AUCKLAND & NORTHLAND

WITH HAURAKI GULF & COROMANDEL

Auckland Harbour Bridge and Westhaven Marina.

Russell, Bay of Islands, Northland.

Photographs, text and design by

PETER MORATH

ISBN: 978-1-877303-53-1

All photographs by the author except where indicated.

Distributed by
Nationwide Book Distributors
www.nationwidebooks.co.nz

and

MF Hunter Holdings
www.hunterholdings.co.nz

and

The Caxton Press
www.caxton.co.nz

Printed by CAXTON Published by The Caxton Press

AUCKLAND & NORTHLAND

WITH HAURAKI GULF & COROMANDEL

Auckland's Westhaven Marina.
Left: Cathedral Cove, Hahei, Coromandel Peninsula.

70

New Zealand's North Island

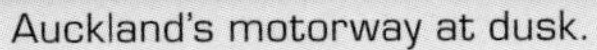
Auckland's motorway at dusk.

One Tree Hill, Auckland.

Roberton Island, Bay of Islands, Northland.

New Zealand has a total population of approximately 4.6 million people. Around 75% live in the North Island as do 90% of Maori, who number 14.3% of the country's citizens. The first European immigrants arrived in 1814 when missionaries established a settlement in the Bay of Islands. Today the Bay is renowned for its big-game fishing and idyllic beaches and is the region's major tourist centre. Northland's industries include oil refining (near its city of Whangarei), farming, fishing and forestry. However, the few giant kauri trees are now protected.

Auckland is home to over a quarter of New Zealand's population. It is recognised as the country's commercial capital and has the largest Polynesian population in the world. This rapidly expanding city is beautifully located on the Waitemata Harbour and within easy reach of the islands of the Hauraki Gulf and the bush-clad mountains and fine beaches of the Waitakere Ranges and Coromandel Peninsula.

To the south is the Waikato region and its thriving dairy industry. Hamilton, its regional centre, is the country's fourth largest city.

The Bay of Plenty is the heart of the kiwifruit industry and Port of Tauranga handles more export cargo than any other in New Zealand. This includes much of the timber grown in the vast forests of the central North Island. The thermal areas of Rotorua, Taupo and the Tongariro National Park provide the North Island's most spectacular sights. Among these are geysers, boiling mud pools and active volcanoes. In winter Mount Ruapehu's ski-fields are an added attraction. The last major eruption in this region was Mount Ruapehu's in 1996.

Eastland is sparsely populated and includes the unspoiled Te Urewera National Park. There is fine coastal scenery around the East Cape north of Gisborne.

Napier and Hastings are the twin cities of the highly productive Hawke's Bay region. Fruit and vegetable growing are major industries, as are wine-making and sheep farming. Napier is renowned for its fine Art Deco buildings.

Taranaki is famous for dairy farming and the production of natural gas and synthetic fuel. The city of New Plymouth is dominated by the beautiful, symmetrical volcano Mount Taranaki in the Egmont National Park.

The the south and south-west lie the predominantly pastoral regions of Whanganui, with its scenic and historic river; Manawatu, with its university city of Palmerston North; and Wairarapa, well known for the Golden Shears sheep-shearing contest held at Masterton.

Wellington has been New Zealand's capital since 1865. It is the country's second largest city, with populations also in the Hutt Valley to the north. It has a magnificent natural harbour from which ferries cross Cook Strait to the South Island.

Left: Auckland Harbour Bridge from Northcote.

AUCKLAND & NORTHLAND

WITH HAURAKI GULF & COROMANDEL

Albert Park, Auckland.

Waiheke Island, Hauraki Gulf.

Mill Bay, Mangonui, Northland.

Auckland city straddles the Auckland Volcanic Field, which has produced 90 volcanic eruptions from 50 volcanoes in the last 90,000 years. These volcanoes are all considered to be extinct, although the volcanic field itself is merely dormant. The city is situated on an isthmus, with Waitemata Habour to the north and Manukau Harbour to the south. Auckland is beautifully situated on the shores of Waitemata Harbour. New Zealand's largest city, it has a population of around 1,416,000, 32% of the country's total, and is acknowledged to be the country's commercial capital. It has the largest Polynesian population in the world. Pasifika people represent 6.9% of the total New Zealand population and 9.2% of that of Auckland. Nearly a quarter of New Zealand's Maori population live in Auckland; they make up 7.8% of the city's inhabitants.

With the harbour and the wide Hauraki Gulf beyond, it is not surprising that sailing plays a large part in many Aucklanders' lives. This has inevitably bred many first class sailors, resulting in Team New Zealand winning the prestigious America's Cup in 1995 and successfully defending it in 2000, when the Louis Vuitton challenger series was held in Auckland. Viaduct Harbour is a hub for more than 30 bars and restaurants, hotels and water-based tourism activities, attracting thousands of visitors annually. Another benefit of its marine location has been that, of the city's many diverse commercial activities, boat building of an international standard is playing a major part.

Many daily commuters also use water transport. Frequent ferry services operate to and from Devonport, used by both tourists and North Shore residents. Other services ply frequently to and from Waiheke Island, also used by commuters and many tourists. Coaches take visitors around the island to see the sights and to sample wines and olives. The gulf has many fascinating islands, most famous of which are Rangitoto and Kawau. The former, a landmark seen across Waitemata Harbour, is the largest of Auckland's volcanoes. It is visible from most parts of the city. Kawau was once the scene of bitter Maori tribal warfare but later became the home of Governor George Grey, whose 'Mansion House' still stands in Mansion House Bay. Manganese and copper used to be mined on this island, which is served by a regular ferry service from Sandspit near Warkworth.

Left: Tairua Harbour from Mount Paku, Coromandel Peninsula.

Pohutukawa trees in bloom at Christmas time in Devonport, Auckland

A two-hour boat service also operates to Coromandel, although most visitors travel to this beautiful peninsula by road. The drive takes about an hour and a half to reach Thames, which is Coromandel's major town, situated at the southern end of the peninsula. There is little doubt that the eastern side of Coromandel Peninsula is the most scenic, from Waihi in the south to Matarangi in the north. There are many fine beaches on this coastline, the best known being Whangamata, Hahei, Hot Water Beach, Whitianga, Waihi Beach and Pauanui with its up-market canal development. Tairua, which is roughly mid-way, makes a delightfully scenic place to stay. There are signs of thermal activity along this coastline, particularly at Hot Water Beach. The bush-clad interior with its forest park and mountain ranges shows many signs of historic volcanic activity. The scenic beauty of this area resembles Pacific islands such as Tahiti. Gold mining was once a major industry and a mine still operates at Waihi.

Northland is one of New Zealand's major tourist areas, in particular the area known as the Bay of Islands, which is steeped in history. The first Maori landing there was in the 10th century and the first

European settlers were missionaries who arrived in 1814. In 1840 the historic Treaty of Waitangi was signed between Maori and the Crown at Waitangi.

Paihia near Waitangi is the centre of tourism in the Bay of Islands, with plentiful accommodation and a fine ferry terminal. From there a frequent service operates across the bay to idyllic Russell, perhaps the best loved destination in the region. Cruises also take visitors to the 'Hole in the Rock' at Peircy Island near Cape Brett. Other cruises operate around the bay and coach trips from Paihia run along the 90 Mile Beach on the west coast up to Cape Reinga, the country's most northerly point. Many of the east coast bays and beaches up north are magnificent; among these are Doubtless Bay and Whangaroa Bay. To the north-west of the Bay of Islands lies Hokianga Harbour with its huge sand dunes and the nearby Waipoua Kauri Forest and Trounson Kauri Park, where some of the tallest and oldest kauri trees are preserved.

To the south lies Dargaville, and across on the east coast is Whangarei, the regional capital. This vibrant centre is situated on the magnificent Whangarei Harbour, with its many bays and fine beaches on both sides. To the east of the city is the beautiful Tutukaka Coast with more lovely harbours and beaches, an area well worth visiting on a day trip from Whangarei.

Auckland's Skytower which stands above the city's casino.

AUCKLAND

Auckland Harbour Bridge and Westhaven Marina with Hauraki and Rangitoto beyond.

Keelers passing Westhaven Marina at the start of a weekend race.
Inset: Westhaven Marina and the Harbour bridge

Some prominent Auckland buildings:
Upper left: The University. **Upper right:** The Art Gallery. **Lower left:** The Museum. **Lower right:** The Town Hall.

Mairangi Bay has one of the east coast's many fine bathing beaches that look towards Rangitoto.

The North Shore, with Devonport and its conical Mount Victoria on the right. On the left, in the distance, is the Royal New Zealand Navy's main base.

Upper left: One Tree Hill. **Upper centre:** Parnell Rose Gardens. **Upper right:** Parnell Village.
Lower: The Tamaki River and Panmure Basin.

Auckland's central business district, with the Hilton Hotel in the foreground and the Skytower at upper right.

HAURAKI GULF

Browns Island is one of the best preserved volcanoes in the Auckland Volcanic Field. It is situated north of Musick Point.
The island in the background is Motutapu, with its artificial causeway link to Rangitoto Island.

Three of the Gulf's islands.
Upper: Rangitoto Island, seen from Tamaki Bay, Auckland. **Lower left:** Pakatoa Island. **Lower right:** Waiheke Island.

Pohutukawas in flower at Oneroa Bay on Waiheke Island.

Mansion House Bay, Kawau Island. 'Mansion House' itself, seen here, was the residence of one of the first Governors of New Zealand, Sir George Grey. Cruises to the Island operate from Auckland and a ferry from Sandspit near Warkworth.

NORTHLAND

Upper: Cape Maria Van Diemen, named by Abel Tasman in 1643. **Lower left:** Cape Reinga Lighthouse. **Lower right:** The Tasman Sea meets the Pacific Ocean at the Cape, in a swirl of currents and a marked colour difference.

Houhora, Great Exhibition Bay.

Taipa, Doubtless Bay.

Coopers Beach, Doubtless Bay.

Mangonui, Doubtless Bay. There is an annual Waterfront Festival held here.

Whangaroa is dominated by the ancient volcanic plug named St Paul's Rock. It is seen at upper left in this picture.
Whangaroa Harbour is one of the finest in the country.

Waipoua Forest near Omapere has some of the finest examples of the few remaining kauri trees.
Left: Waipoua's 51m high 'Tane Mahuta' ('King of the Forest') is estimated to be aged between 1200 and 2500 years. **Right:** The 'Darby and Joan' kauri.

Hokianga Harbour from above Omapere. The vast sand dunes on the north side of the Harbour are a notable feature.

Historic Kerikeri Inlet in the Bay of Islands was established as a mission station in 1819 by Samuel Marsden. The Stone Store seen here was built in 1835 and is still trading. The Inlet is a popular mooring area for yachts.

Waitangi, with the historic Treaty Ground, which can be seen at centre right with its flagpole.

Sunrise over Waitangi boat harbour.
Left inset: Waitangi Meeting House. **Right inset:** Waitangi Treaty House.

Christ Church, Russell is the country's oldest.

Left: Russell is perhaps the best known of the Bay of Island's resorts. Steeped in history, it was the seat of government until 1841. It is hard to believe that this idyllic place was once known as the 'Hell-Hole of the Pacific', so numerous were its grog shops and houses of ill repute. This aerial view looks south.

This aerial view of the Russell area faces north. The main township is on the left with Matauwhi Bay in the foreground.

Paihia is the principal tourism centre in the Bay of Islands. Accommodation is plentiful and a ferry service to Russell and other cruises operate from the fine boat terminal. **Inset**: The Bay of Islands is renowned for big-game fishing.

Upper: One of the most popular cruises from Paihia is through the 'Hole in the Rock' at Piercy Island.
Lower left: Kayaking at Haruru Falls near Paihia. **Lower right:** Holiday makers enjoying the sunshine on Paihia beach.

Two of the several fine beaches on Moturua Island.
Inset: The Bay of Islands is a superb location for sailing.

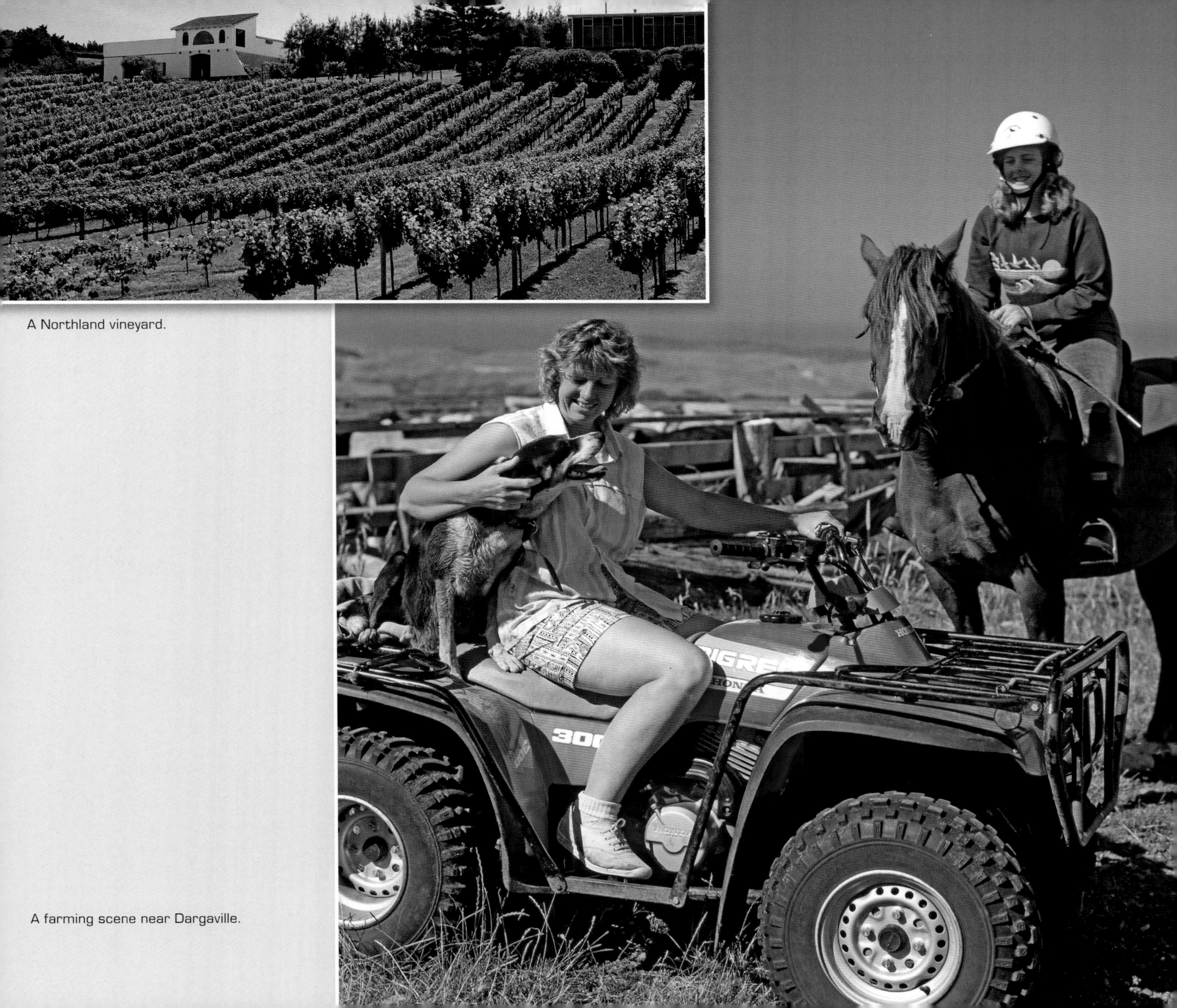
A Northland vineyard.

A farming scene near Dargaville.

Whangarei is the northernmost city in New Zealand and regional capital of Northland.
This view is of the city's attractive Town Basin.

A mixed herd of cattle grazing the lower slopes of Mount Manaia on Whangarei Harbour.

A Hereford herd grazing contentedly at the delightful little settlement of Pataua on Ngunguru Bay near Whangarei.

Upper left: Whangarei Harbour with Bream Head and Lion Head in the distance. **Upper right:** Matapouri Beach, Tutukaka Coast. **Lower left:** Ngunguru, Tutukaka Coast. **Lower right:** Sheltered Bay, Tutukaka Coast.

Tutukaka Harbour north of Whangarei. This is a very popular boating area with a fine marina at Tutukaka. Big-game fishing trips operate from here.

Piha in the Waitakere Ranges on the south-west coast of Northland, with Lion Rock on the left.
It has one of the North Island's best surfing beaches.

Ruakaka on Bream Bay south of Whangarei. The Bay has fine, sandy beaches and Waipu further south is a popular holiday location.

Langs Beach, near Ruakaka, Bream Bay.

COROMANDEL

Dairy farming in the beautiful countryside near Hikuai, south-west of Pauanui in east Coromandel.

Whangamata on the east coast, one of Coromandel's principal holiday resorts.

A section of the superb eastern coastline of Coromandel near Hahei.
Inset: Te Horo Rock at Cathedral Cove near Hahei.

Pauanui near Tairua from Mount Paku.

Sunset over Tairua Harbour, one of Coromandel's most scenic locations, seen here from Mount Paku.